Ribcage
WINNER OF THE 2015 KITHARA BOOK PRIZE

RIBCAGE
Joan Colby

GLASS LYRE PRESS

Copyright © 2015 Joan Colby
Paperback ISBN: 978-1-941783-08-5

All rights reserved: except for the purpose of quoting brief passages for review, no part of this book may be reproduced or transmitted in any form or by any means, electronic or mechanical, including photocopying, recording, or by any information storage and retrieval system, without permission in writing from the publisher.

Cover art & design: Melinda B Hipple
Interior design & layout: Steven Asmussen
Copyediting: Elizabeth Nichols
Author Photo: FourFootedFotos

Glass Lyre Press, LLC
P.O. Box 2693
Glenview, IL 60026

www.GlassLyrePress.com

RIBCAGE
winner of the 2015 Kithara Book Prize

The *kithara* was an ancient Greek musical instrument in the lyre family used for solo playing, as well as to accompany poetry and song.

Previous Winners

2013 — *Idyll for a Vanishing River* by Jeffrey C. Alfier
2014 — *Cephalopodic* by J.P. Dancing Bear

Contents

All the Red Horses	17
In Which the Heart Takes Ease	19
Running Red and Hopeless	20
Concealed Architecture	21
Sucked from the Throats of Virgins	22
Hummingbirds of the Involuntary System	24
War Canoes upon the Outposts	25
Hammers and Anvils	26
Kneeling like Field Hands	27
Bald as the Old God	29
Stalled in the Cosmos	30
Cached in a Locket	32
Constricted with Morpheus	34
Vertigo of Misrule	35
Betray with Imprint	36
Prophets and Blasphemers	37
Red and White Signifiers	38
Coughing up Roses	39
Serpents of Courage	41
Commas of the Complex Sentence	42
Lights and Sirens	43
Territory of Robbed Stagecoaches	44
Cobra Venom in the Heart	45
Transmuted to Gold	46
Chewed to Meat Hooks	47
Fit and Nervy	49
Envelope of Servitude	50
Bleeding into Satin	52
The Body as Metaphor: Poetry in the Schools	53
Derivation of the Word	57
"and speech created thought"	58
Incantations	60

Who	61
What	62
Where	63
Why	64
When	65
The Nature of Freedom	66
Déjà Vu	67
Meditation Stroll	68
Fugue	69
Subjects	70
Visitations	71
Passwords	72
Crow Song	74
Aria	75
The Japanese Gardens	76
The Herd of Stars	78
Soft Spot	79
Correlations	80
Cold Prophecies	81
Homeward	82
Tulips	83
Vanessa Atalanta	85
Wild Strawberries	86
Composing the Essay	87
The Coming of Blindness	88
Tea Rose	90
Bridal Wreath	91
Apparitions of Earth	92

For Aislen who must carry the torch...

Acknowledgments

These poems, some in other versions, have appeared in the following journals: *After Hours, Anemone, Apeiron Review, Atlanta Review, Avocet, Big River Poetry Review, Blue Bear Review, Broadkill Review, Calliope, Caveat Lector, Chiron Review, Cider Press Review, Dead Snakes, Homestead Review, Interim, Kansas Quarterly, Kentucky Review, Misfitmagazine, Mojave River Review, Monterey Poetry Journal, Muddy River Poetry Review, New Stone Circle, Nimrod, One, The Pedestal, Pirene's Fountain, Reed Magazine, Slant, South Dakota Review, Squeezebox, 10X3 Plus, Turtle Island Poetry Review, Verse Wisconsin, Windless Orchard.*

Special thanks to consummate editor Ami Kaye whose support is appreciated more than I can say.

The Body in Question

All the Red Horses

It keeps squeezing
Eagerly, a deformed hand
Seeking the flesh of its desire.
The lungs are giant ears that open and shut
Upon the heart's primitive word.
A word that has one syllable,
One note
Echoing the monotone that throbs
Deep in the ocean and the rock.

When the body runs
The heart pursues it
Its red cloak flying.

When the body sleeps
The heart soothes it
With the steady stroke
Of a rower through calm waters.

When the body makes love
The heart stands up in its boat
Rocking dangerously
As the current takes it
To the brink of the waterfall.

The heart never rests,
It drives the body unheeded,
A teamster urging
All the red horses
Day and night, day and night.

When the body betrays it
The heart grows
Enormous and flaccid,
A fat and sulking creature
On a grey porch,
Rocking and halting, rocking and halting,
Biding its time.

In Which the Heart Takes Ease

Harp that strums with the soul
Of harmony. Haunting curve of bone.
The sweetest meat. Here's where breath
And meter meet. The drum of pulse,
A scarlet tanager.

Shaped to cage the shudder
Of a caught bird, temptesuous.
A flutter of red wings.
Arias of frost or melt,
The burning absolutions of
A turning season. Here's
The crafted Windsor chair in which
The heart takes ease. Remember

How woman sprang from rib
As man slept unaware. The delicate
Bend like willows, like the
Compromise of love.

Running Red and Hopeless

Its capacity for holding in
The vulnerable
And harmonious organs.

Egyptian priests preserved it
Oiled and wrapped like cocoons.
After George Parrott, the train robber,
Was hanged, Doc Osborne had him
Skinned and tanned
Into a pair of fine leather shoes.
The Nazis made lampshades
From the skins of Jews.

In "The Trees" Richter describes
Indians skinning a captured
Wolf, letting it run red
And hopeless into the woods
While they jeered drunk
On white man's whiskey.

As we age, our skin thins,
Its map splotches with destroyed cities.
The continent of the self erodes.
Theologians insist our bodies
Will arise on the Last Day
In wondrous skins of belief.

Concealed Architecture

I broke the first ones at eleven
Falling off a high embankment
Onto a roadway. Tibia and ankle.
A cast to my hip covered in the
Graffiti of signatures.

Later, wrists, collarbones, the fifth
Metatarsal, the most commonly broken.
Femur screwed to a steel plate
And bolted to the hip.

Old bones. My mother shrinking
Into half a parenthesis. The bones
Fusing. Or Ron, his spine
Rebuilt with cadaver bone,
A half corpse until he shot himself.

The x-ray seeks them. The diagram
Of concealed architecture. Modern
Art, stark as Modigliani or staggered
As a Picasso nude on the stairs.

You say you can't float,
Bones heavy as a mastodons.
Big feet, shoulders equipped
For burden. My bones are sparrows.
I could lie back forever in the ocean
And be carried. They must be hollow
To snap so easily, like dry retorts.

My fat friend has the last laugh.
Hauling all that lard all these years,
Her bones are strong as masts.
As beams that hold a house up.

Sucked from the Throats of Virgins

A delta on the back of my hand
Fed by blue tributaries that course
Over wrist bones. Within, the red
Rivers run.

Like a limestone subtstrate, the body
Is undercut with subterranean
Waters. Cells that pool and disperse.
The brain can submerge
Like a car in a flooded viaduct. Or a barge
Stuck in a lock can shock
All passage into collapse. So much

Can go wrong. Bad blood thought
To cause syphilis, the failed marrow,
Uncontrolled ravages of leukemia.
Old tactics of leeches.

There are those who can't abide
The sight of blood and those
Who fly through windows at night
To suck it from the throats of virgins.
A hunter at his first kill
Is smeared: blooded.

Mine is the blood of the universal
Donor—O-negative.
I give you blood. Your blood
Would kill me.
The traces that betray
The murderer.

Sangre de Cristo, transubstantiations.
An old story, how we might change.
Those little fountains pulsing
With every heartbeat.

Hummingbirds of the Involuntary System

A tapestry of snakes and vines,
Tendrils that wind like blue rivers
Through the landscape of the body.
Small canoes with sensational cargoes,
Wicker baskets of fruit and flowers.
The fibers of motion quiver, hummingbirds
Of the involuntary system. Numbness attends
Injury, the godmother of healing, until the
Nerves awaken like wolves to howl
Down a crescent moon.
Relapsing disease unsheaths the
Silver bullets spilling into dust
And no one is safe now. The spinal cord
Severed as the rider falls, all spotlights
Flickering and failing. A dark and snowbound
Dwelling. Think of the woman who finally cracks
Like bad plaster, arroyos of despair. The outdated
Diagnosis: nervous breakdown: the blown fuses
Sparking and shutting down. Hair
Wild with neglect and eyes claret
With premonition.

War Canoes upon the Outposts

Guard towers on the secret rivers
Where currents run white as a
Bivouacked army. Watchful as shepherds
Clocking each intrusion
With raised staffs or tonsured
Monks standing in hermitages
Of silent petition. Caretakers
Of the sacred mysteries: how life
Is blessed.
Pure relief of the negative proposition,
No renegade cells launching
War canoes upon the outposts,
No imperialist colonies
Ravaging the precious ores,
The mahogany forests, the aquafers.
O sentinels of devotion
Sleepless as the body sleeps
In this tireless benevolence,
Swelling to dispel pathogens.
Jealous lovers of the unwary self.

Hammers and Anvils

Pumping iron to steel,
Biceps into chunks of ore,
Breastplates of pectorals,
Titanium grip of quadriceps.
The gym clangs with barbells,
Treadmills, Metallica
Blaring into headphones.

Smooth snaky muscles of the involuntary
Systems: digestion, inspiration, heart.
Skeletal muscles bulging with locomotion.
On steroids, a tide of lactic acid.

Bundles within bundles like
Russian dolls to hold the framework
In perfect contractions.

The dissolving fibers
As if a macramé hanging
Had been shredded by ravens.

Kneeling like Field Hands

Comical as puppets
Enabling the angles of dance and piety. The folded
Contritions of love, articulating
The industry of dianthrosis,
Flopping or waving like someone
In need of rescue.

The elbow designed for nudging,
Black humor of the funny bone.

The knee dimpled like a silent screen star.
Housemaid, scrubwoman, nun.
Pilgrims crawling to the shrine,

The hip permits sitting,
Women at sewing machines
In the locked factory.
Accountants at ledgers,
Pasha content on a fat cushion.

The hip sinuous in the rhumba,
Its gates securing the harem
Of the buttocks. Fleshy veiled women
Luscious with sequestration.

How joints segue from straight
To curve like roads to paradise
Or perdition. Jolly as taverns
Where the unbending idols are smashed.
Oiled with synovial fluids
Like good machines or bone on bone
Scraping the wallpaper of pain.

How simulacrum of ball and socket
Engages the body
Like a second wife, young
And full of spirit.

Bald as the Old God

Noggin of notions that bloom
Like poppies in the fields of the
Frontal cortex. Cultivated,
Inspired. The head upon its stalk
Like a rattling gourd or the sunflower
That drove Van Gogh to suicide.
Tiara, headdress, white Stetson,
Black beret. Signifiers of who's heading what.
Or where. The head leads with its
Eyes set deep as emeralds. A
Predatory impulsion. Thatched
Like the roof of the witch's cottage
Or bald as the old god in his tabernacle.
A child comes headfirst from the womb
Crowning into the crow of light. Swivel
To see peripheries of danger or beauty. The mind
In its maze seeking the thread
Theseus gripped to find the way.
In the first garden they could not yet
Understand that beheading is how you
Kill the snake. The Terror
Designed the guillotine. The shrunken heads
Of defeated warriors. Masked executioner on TV,
A kneeling hostage recites a script. O heads
Of state, flat heads of unattended infants, heads
Suspended in lockets or flash-frozen awaiting
The miracle of science. The one who signs
The register, head of the household. The Red
Queen shouting

Stalled in the Cosmos

Her gestures, that strange salute
To an invisible interrogator,
Were, the neurologist said, due to degeneration
Of the frontal lobe. Which controls
Movement. She says it makes her feel
Better. She's 92. This is what happens.
At least her memory is intact,
The synapses like little space ships
Flying from neuron to neuron.

When I can't recall a word, I think of that
Silvery shape stalled in the cosmos, a time warp
Or a veil of poisonous fog Then: flash it lands
And I know.

In the test of right or left brained, I was a perfect
Centrist. You'd think that would be good, but
No. Impossible decisions
Like hovercraft that have lost direction
Or altitude. A wire-walker stuck
In the art of balance.

The myelin sheath thins and you can no longer walk.
A failure of dopamine and you can no longer sing.
A stroke flooding or clotting until you are
One-sided as a politician.
A mistake in DNA and at the age of forty
You begin to shake and stagger.
You wave your arms.

A woman with breast cancer has them cut off
The way you'd take down a tree
That threatened the house. But the bad cells
Like burglars climbed through hot wires of ganglia
To squat in the parlor of the cerebellum
Spraying tendrils of graffiti.

Grey matter. This sour pudding.
This stuffing in our heads.
This is all we have to reason with.
This balled up dust and hair from under the bed.

Cached in a Locket

See how the infant smiles to evoke
A sympathy of attachment. The uncanny symmetry
Of eyes, the nose, a central talisman,
And lips that open to soothe,
Close on a scold like lids.

Faces bloom in the sweat of plaster,
Or emerge fiercely on tree trunks.
Saints or saviors float in the sky. Green Man
In the wood, virgin in the grotto.
A demon in a straw mask
From Merida.

Faces in old portraits serious
With the business of existence,
Jack-o-lantern faces terrify the child
who draws a kindly circle
With holes for eyes and nostrils and
A curved line that smiles.

Malleable face with pretensions
Of perfection or mockery—
Grimacing, eye-crossed, tongue protruding.
With a dangling rattlestring
On the wall of a Mayan temple.

In death, the face is waxen. Its eyes
Stuck open, mouth agape
With the final breath.

Believer, you stand before these faces:
The smirking moon,
The genial sun,
The indifferent stars,
Seeking, forever seeking
The inscrutable face of god.

Constricted with Morpheus

Three veils, Salome dances
In cornea, uvea, retina, the miracle
Of sight like a cherished head
On a silver platter. The short-sighted
Peer through spectacles
At a diminishing world, presbyopia
Where small print blurs
To a nest of insects, road signs
Leading to dead ends. The astigmatic
Distortions, how love so easily
Misdirects the impassioned and far-sight
Becomes useless, a wounded hawk.
Even in slumber, the eyes are unquiet
With vivid dreams forsaken by
The wakeful. How pupils constrict
With Morpheus, the sleep-giver, or
Enlarge with a lover's touch.
Oedipus put out his eyes when he discovered
Jocasta's identity, and stumbled blind
With guilt, blind
As Helen learning words by feeling,
A hand cupping water. The vitreous floaters
Sail their rafts across the sightlines
Of the aging who blink and blink
To restore focus. The cataracts that form
Like a stream finding its way
To a geology of falling.
Blue, brown, green, gray, the iris
Evokes lyric. The aqueous humour.
Tear ducts that release
All the grief we can't endure.

Vertigo of Misrule

A labyrinth implies loss
Clinging to a thread as bird song
Vanishes, the aria blocked
At the gate of the high C.

At 26, Beethoven began
To learn how rising frequencies
Caught in the epithelium
Of dazed hair cells might falter.
When he could no longer
Hear the music nor the applause,
His thoughts turned to suicide.
The temporal bone
Dense with the memory of speech.

The seat of balance
In the vestibular hall engages justice.
How vertigo can spin the body
Into misrule, how tinnitus
Clamours like petitioners, the Eustachian tube
Clacking like a nun at her beads.
Whispering snail of the cochlea.

The ear lobe invested with
Decoration. Pierced with the golden ring
A carousel rider grabs
Hoping for luck. The way the ears
Of captives strung on cords
Darken to an amber that reveals
The fossils of heartbreak.

Betray with Imprint

The dermatologist says her lips
Are voluptuous. The Cupid's bow
Of Clara's charm, now Botox
Plumps like memory foam.
Lacquered red or softened pink
As a Gibson Girl. Pucker
To kiss, thin to condemn.
Betray with imprint on
Collar or cheek. Hot lips.
How they harbor teeth, form the phrases
Of love and denial. A gun moll told
Don't give me lip in a thirties' noir
Flick. Fat lip of abuse. Lip
Service of lobbyists or magicians
On the lip of something stupendous.
Bite your lip,
Shy child as you learn
What you must withhold.

Prophets and Blasphemers

Red boat of taste, it explores
Seas of savory and salt,
Grieves like a mermaid in waters
Churning from sweet to bitter.
Inspector of crevices, soul kiss
And nipple. The worm of desire.
Intimate eel. It slips
In a Freudian alley, waltzes in
Irony cheek to cheek.
Bitten to vanquish the slur,
It bleeds like the Sacred Heart
Hung over the bed to warn
Lovers who lick the crumbs.
See how it roves in the cage
Of bicuspids and molars. A map
Of arroyos, it roots at the edge
Of a gulf to lap pieties
Or project the insults of a
Scarlet child. Gustatory muscle of
Prophets and blasphemers,
Incarnate with the rage
Of peppery notions. Incantations
Cartwheeling like tumbleweeds.
Choirs of papillae
Silent for eons, the tongue
In its cave like a snake
Anticipating the word
That unlatches the gates
Into a world of temptation.

Red and White Signifiers

The uvula hangs at the doorway,
A bell full of gutterals,
The click consonants of a minor tribe.
Plunger of vibrations,
Old man, mouth ajar, snoring.

The Palatine guards of the tonsils
Stand in the village of childhood
Where the red and white signifiers
Invoke the ether mask, and then
The knife. It was unnecessary,
That's today's opinion. The untonsiled
Of a particular age know
The cycles of ignorance.

A bird in its cage, the larynx harbors song,
Grows hoarse with nodules,
Loses range. The pure soprano
Reaches for the high note and squawks
Like an untested microphone.

The epiglottis, that clapper, saves us
From drowning in our drink. A first
Responder to all that goes down wrong.

The bee sting, the pill, the rogue peanut
Swells the throat trapping breath
Like a bear in a cave with the savages
Waving torches.

It is the throat the strangler loves.
The throat on which the noose
Of thirteen coils will close.

Coughing up Roses

Soaring like turkey vultures
On the updrafts, effortlessly,
Beneath notice, how the diaphragm
Squeezes them into the gymnastic
Arts of expiration, inspiration.
Bald red pistons. Fraternal twins.

A cigarette butt discarded on our drive.
Someone whose lungs are scarred
As if lashed at the mast. The coughing fit,
Morning hack and spit. A woman
In the restroom taking a final drag. Tomorrow
The surgery. She still loves it
The way a beaten woman loves the man
Who weeps drunkenly in her lap
Swearing he'll stop.

The lungers; Keats, Mansfield, Lawrence,
Doc Holliday. The white plague
Of the Magic Mountain. Camille
On her chaise. The Bronte sisters
Coughing up roses.

Pneumonia, the old man's friend,
Settling in like a vagrant
In a foreclosed house
Pulling a wooly blanket over his head.

O bellows of existence.
The ins and outs. The dreaded spot
Or the vast capacity
Of the long-distance swimmer.

The lobes pumping your calves
To cycle uphill struggling
For breath. Breath in the aleveoli circling
Like a kettle of vultures.

Say it. The old word. Buzzards
Perched on the bedrail as you draw
The last rattling lungfull.

Serpents of Courage

After Eden, the snake coiled
In the belly of mankind, its grey
Revolutions digesting the essence
Of what we would become:
A creature of appetites.

The pain after a hearty meal,
Like grief that follows the act of love.

The windings
Of the interior, blind canyons,
Passages narrow enough to foil spelunkers.
The photographs of the ruined city.
The all-clear after the raid.

To be drawn and quartered, that's a sentence
For traitors. Hung, cut down
Still living. The ropes of intestine
Hauled out and burned. The livid crowd
Cranes forward, cheers.

Gutshot, a man dies slowly
In anguish. A hunter tracks
Such animals to end the misery.
After battle, a screaming corporal
Clasps his ripped belly, is offered
Water, a cigarette, with luck morphine.

The serpents of courage
Hibernate in the gut.
Each man is tested as they wake
Hissing from a long winter of peace.

COMMAS OF THE COMPLEX SENTENCE

Kidneys. Two cheerful siblings working in tandem
Like Jack and Jill with their pails.
Commas in the complex sentence
Of the body. Beans or boomerangs.

Imagine, how a part of yourself can depart
To settle in the continent of a stranger.
This cashew of your interior.
Sweet laundress of the bloodstream.

Lights and Sirens

It's a worm, that vestigial organ.
In that long-ago when men
Were starting to grow upright
With elongated skulls, it helped them
Digest the stalky plants. Now it's useless,
Yet lethal. Acclaimed with
Lights and sirens.

1735, an eleven year old boy
swallowed a pin, the first
To be saved by its removal.
In 1961, Dr. Leonid Rogozov
At a remote Antarctic base,
Operated on himself, to be awarded
The Order of the Red Banner of Labor.

Territory of Robbed Stagecoaches

Nestled like a slug into the stomach's
Mermaid curve. Or an infant cuddled
In the madonna's arms.
Like miners laboring in the interior
Of salt domes or coal seams, here's where
The significant activity occurs.

Travel to the islets of Langerhorn
A pirate's haven, cells clustered with ransom.
Enzymes of buried treasure. Insulin of need.
Ambiguity of sugars. Born into a territory
Of robbed stagecoaches or rich
With the treacherous fats of the land.

Measure blood the way an assayer
Weighs ore. Toes blackening to basalt,
The Precambrian shield
Where men with scalpels gather.

Cobra Venom in the Heart

Sea slug filtering blood.
Another organ one can live without.
The ancient Greeks proclaimed it
One of the Humors: Melancholy.
It vents black bile like a demon,
Spits its cobra venom in your heart
Until all you feel is rage—
A poison you take willingly.

Transmuted to Gold

The sonorous dirge of wrath, jealousy and greed
Reverberate in this, the largest of visceral organs.
Dark lobes like giant salamanders. The bilary flow.

Busy as an engineer
Metabolizing, storing, detoxing
As we swill Martinis
In the chambers of cirrhosis.

Fired up for regeneration
As Prometheus and the eagle
Describe compensatory growth,
How an anole's snapped-off tail
Renews, how a soul can be saved
By faith or works.
Transmuted to gold like the mask
Of a pharaoh.

Chewed to Meat Hooks

If the index finer is shorter than the ring finger
It means something. I forget what.
My index finger bears a scar at the knuckle
Where a paring knife carved a half moon
Red as harvest.

The ring finger wedded in gold, signals
Constancy. Has no particular function
Other than grip.

The pinkie, choice of mobsters or the studly
For an ostentatious gemstone. O little one
Heavy with attitude.

The opposable dwarf whose magic
Shapes art or industry. Thumbs up
For the short and the ugly.
The portly judge.

Which leads us to the signifier
Insolent as a poker. To be used
For motorists who cut me off.

The white-capped fingernails
Tough as riptides. As a child
I chewed them to their
Meat hooks. A solace
Mutilation can provide.

Five digits
Swarming from the palm,
Each independent as a burglar.

And the palm, that continent of platitudes—
Rivers of mind and heart and fate.
The lifeline you cling to,
How it runs off the edge of the map
To a wilderness from which no one returns.

Fit and Nervy

A panorama of giant sculpted legs
Overlooks the lakefront, standing firm
Against the elements, brainless but baleful.
Bronze thighs, thick calves
Of soccer players, muscled, indelicate.
Pinup of the forties, Betty Grable's fabled gams
Insured for a million bucks. Long legged ladies
Of wet dreams. Liz Taylor's too short
And plump, Burton laughed defusing
The myth of eternal beauty, a self
That challenged his. The way an amputee
Senses the absent limb. At Fredericksburg
Piles of legs piled up outside the surgeon's tent.
Whitman wept and comforted the men
Whose peglegs would prop them like pirates.
Legs Diamond was an expert
At the tango. A bootlegger to boot.
Bow legs or piano legs, the spread legs
Of the willing, the way you leg up
A horse, fit and nervy. A rumor: how the pious
Politician got a leg over
Goes viral, has legs. He wants to leg it
From screens and mobiles, from the
Headlines black legends. Legs.
Preposterous forked emblems
Of symmetry. The old jockeys say
It is the legs that give out first.

Envelope of Servitude

Twenty-eight bones. The fifth metatarsal
The most frequently fractured. Bearing
The weight of the body
Like a pack mule laden
With gold dust. Bare, it forms
The hoof of a callous.
Confined it learns the audacity
Of fashion. Bunions like burls
Of an oak. Corns squeezed with the
Pointed toes of stillettos. The Chinese
Declared a big foot offensive,
Folded the insteps of girls
Into the envelope of servitude.
Half the Union army went barefoot
Into battle, their provisioned shoes rotting.
Half the women of the world
Soak their tired feet at night.
Others flip-flop unceremoniously,
A strap harnessing toes
Like a five-in-hand
Hauling the coach of vertical
Ambition. The flat foot that saves a man
From gunfire. The high arch of
Social mobility. Here's one who loves
The foot beyond comprehension,
Sucking the toes, collecting the shapely
Slippers as if what supported the body
In its upright version must be worshipped.
How the club foot lamed Byron
Into an excess of poetry. Achilles'
Vulnerability, tendon the wolf seizes
To eat its prey alive. Mary, armed

With a halo, foot upon the serpent, preparing
To ascend into the realm of the footless.

Bleeding into Satin

Ingrown nail festers, overripe
As an overlooked fruit,
Red and hot. The shoe
That fits is the one you cannot bear.
Clip straight or else the wear
And tear of footfalls will suspend
Pace. How the meter of stride
Depends on grace.
Thickening with age, yellow as a gourd.
Witchery pump or fuck-me spikes amend
To hammertoe, crossover bunion. Five
Chubby pigs hurrying to market. The
Ballerina bleeds into satin,
Art hugs pain. The horse runs
Upon stiffened toes horny as an old
Man's lust. Betrayal of the stubbed,
Tiptoeing past the locked door. The cry.
The sugar rot, black as bad meat. Sweet
Appendage to toe the mark.

The Body as Metaphor: Poetry in the Schools

David says the heart is in a jail.
Melody says eyes
Are mirrors in which a person sees
The colors of the self.
Emilee says hair
Is a mutiny. Paul tells how bones
Keep us from falling apart.
Robert wants to know
If the spleen is a blood factory.
Jodie raises her hand which is a claw.
Philip says knees allow
A man to bend. Jennifer
Says veins are tracks on which
The blue trains race crammed with
Bloodshot eyes. Susan remembers tears
Are rain that salts the earth
Until nothing more can thrive.
Derrick says his fist
Is the animal on the cave wall
Bristling with spears.
Cara says her skin
Keeps everything, everything
Within. Linda thinks her lungs
Are giant ears of eavesdroppers.
Brian, who is blind,
Says the tongue is a prisoner. Teach it
To be kind.

The Mind at Play

Derivation of the Word

It began as sacrifice.
The favored son. The virgin.
A chalice of blood: blod.

Then surrogates: ram or doe.
The prettiness
Of a lamb.

A market to purchase doves.
Priests whose knives make holy
These supplications: bledsion.

Softened in time to blessen.
A votive candle instead.
Blessing.

Said over the Sunday roast
Or like a gift of good will
Bestowed.

"AND SPEECH CREATED THOUGHT"

I waken
Consumed with heat
Though the windows are blind with frost
And ice creaks the trees
Like the bellows of an organ
Fallen into disuse.

It's getting light. I reach
For the copy of Shelley
I fell asleep upon,
Read *and speech created thought*
And think of the ape's larynx
Which won't permit more than the crudest mimic
Of man's repertoire.

A zoo of eyes
Stares pathetically between the bars
Of the evolutionary chart
Expressing mainly the fear
Of creatures who devise their lives
From utterances like these.

And speech created thought
Which is the measure of the universe
Shelley, radical, disbeliever,
Believer, enamored of crackpot
Notions and great ideas,
Convulsing yourself with nightmare tales,
Gothic free-lover,
Theorist, good friend,
Startling the future
With this image of atomic matter—

Orbs in the sphere
Upon a thousand sightless axles spinning
Or your vision of electricity as the new
Promethean fire that *walks through fields*
Or cities while men sleep.

Incantations

Twisted forest light compels
An utterance of druids
Blue as agony.

A magpie reveres
Its treasures,
Tinfoil, a copper coin.

Think of the brigandry
Of crows. Crazed speech
That etches glass.

How priests
Raise chalices full of
Dead language.

Women whisper behind
Onyx rings. They want to tell
Unspeakable things.

The cant of politicians
Paints the wall with duplicity
Cowering like a cat boys have stoned.

Sweet ejaculations sever
Years of burning. Come close, I'll
Show you what a spell is.

Who

Who spots the golden eye of the lynx
Or the mushroom nestled in the oak root.
Who posits the dictum *I am, therefore I think*
In a reverse Descartes, a sort of brute
Ideology mastering the animate nation.

Who envisions the way the lake
Ripples in the forenoon like a shed skin.
Who first praised the rattlesnake's
Divinity, the way it can move in
And out of itself, a self creation.

Who took the maiden's hand,
Who led her to the sacred well
Where bones bleached into a command
For rain that, for ages, never fell.
Who celebrated then, with what elation.

What

What translates the language of the rain
On rooftops on a Tuesday morning.
What calculates the images of fame
Or billows with cumulonimbus warning
Like storms clenching right at the horizon.

What mimics the footfalls of the small
Creatures or the hoofbeats of the horses.
What can we learn from the terrible
Patterns of the wind or watercourses
Braiding to a portentous liaison.

What happens when the curtains start to sway
What luminosity can be affected
In a moment that's an hour, then a day
So everything we knew is indirected
And diffuse, a kind of gauzy prison.

Where

Where did the footprints lead
Where was the forest path we sought
In the painting by Renoir. The seed
Of philosophy is withering and fraught
With bad desires, a pond of algae.

Where else can the storied gold be hid
Sacred mountains and rainbows are a child's
Fantasy—a kettle with no lid
Where everything boils, tame and wild
A deafened ear, a defective eye.

Where is the church of the possible
The anteroom where everyone kneels
The voices raised in a spurious gospel
Where the statues bless and the bell peels
And the sacrament is merely a sigh

Why

Why even ask this question
Or any question, answers are like mist
Over a river or the incessant
Reasons behind the Judas kiss.
Why betray ourselves or each other.

Why double back when the path is clear
Why second guess every second thought.
The wood is dark, the fox the deer
In silent bowers. Why calculate the cost
Of love, its aptitude to smother.

Why examine the nuance of each sentence
The breakbone evidence of plow on clod.
Why save a talisman for remembrance
Or speculate on if there is a god
How that could impact any lover.

When

When all the barns have collapsed
When windfall apples rot in a gorge of bees
When hollow trees creak in every synapse
Of weather and splitting let the fence wires seize
The edges of the unoccupied pastures.

When fields rise up again in native grasses
And cultivation is an aborted birth
When buffalo emerge from mountain passes
Like ghostly dreams drummed out of the earth
Invisibly, spirits of vanquished textures

When rain falls constantly or not at all
When fires consume the prairies and the slopes
Of foothills where witchlike figures in a caul
Of ash stand like emblems of our various hopes
Making jagged vaguely obscene gestures.

When dark or light is now or never
And you and I are gone forever.

The Nature of Freedom

An open door is terrifying.
Hauls the eye to blue distances,
Roads narrowing like arrowheads,
A sky soaring with birds of prey.

A closed door cannot be borne.
The heart knocks on it. Beats a key
Of breath into shape. Fits it as one
Body fits another. The door
Slides open. Lovers fall apart.
Everything spreads, amorphous,
Uncontained.

Thus: strategy of a window.
Before it, a table,
A book face-down.
Iris in a glass vase.

Outside, a dead
Garden. Bent rake.
An elm
Dressed in rain.

Déja Vu

The pears have ripened.
They are firm as idols.
Every branch makes obeisance
To its fruit. A light wind
Holds the gold flesh in its fingers.
The stems neither glue themselves
Fiercely nor do they break at touch.
Their adhesion is now perfect.
The time of this phenomenon is brief
Next week will see
Windfall rivers in mottled light.
The pure scent of pears
Like fairest flesh, like clearest water,
Suffused with the antique odor
Of love beginning to bruise.

We walk through the pear orchard.
Summer is almost over.
The nights are cooler.
The trees shudder with golden tears
As if a goddess in the root
Whispered of waste and winter.
An oracle
Mists along the distant river.
Its truths go up in smoke.
We have been here.
We have been here.

Meditation Stroll

Stones define the path,
At first a spiral, then curving
Upon itself like the earth, a circle,
The universal prayer of stars and planets.

I am to walk cleaning my mind of notions,
Ideas, reverie, but the whisper of a poem dictates
Its small insistent rhymes
That I long to assemble. They too
Must be lost if I am to complete
This devotion. To unlock memory and then
Dispel it as one departs from a house
That will be demolished,
Taking nothing, leaving it all behind.

I am not adept at this. The hoofs of my
Imagination trotting a familiar road
As I try to follow this confusion,
This whirligig without ending like a poem
That offers no resolution.

This pattern is designed
For peace, I suppose. If I could cease
Thinking. Become the stillness of
A vessel emptied of water. I lack
A lack of impulsion.

Here is the lotus where Lord Krishna
Hovers in his bee-form. I should take no
Notice. But I buzz in the hive of myself.
Honeycomb. Sweet. Sweet.

Fugue

Lopsided music.
All vowels
Like an unspeakable infant.

Blank book of dreams.
Frenzy of branches in the night
Swatting the moon's razor.

Clues to a mystery
In which a body is found
Unmarked.

Victorians photographed
The Ripper's victim
To capture his maimed image

In her pupils. There
Was nothing. Nothing
Is better than silence

Even this distorted music
Beating the air
Into a pattern of twisted silver.

Counterpoint to something.
Age hauls a mirror
Into decline as rain does windows

Falling through fingers, nerves, ganglia,
The brain stem peels off
One feeling after another.

Subjects
after Wislawa Szymborska

No more poems
Are to be written about spring.
Ordinary subjects are blessed:
Inkwells or eggs. An emerald ring.

Only the most adroit shall tackle
The large abstractions:
Truth, beauty, justice.

So we turn to the visible
Such as a fingernail
In which a sun rises
Or sets in a cuticle of flesh.

A faded towel hangs from a rack
Disconsolate as an abbess
Accused of sorcery.

A question mark's
Hook and eye
That will never catch

Never achieve the perfection
Of an answer that can't
Be questioned.

Seize river stones that drying
Have lost all luster.
Remember how they glistened
As the waters lapped and find
Words to bring that back.

Visitations

The days lengthen, then the stria of nightfall:
Dusk, twilight, dark. Stars knitting mythologies.
Moth wings erasing the windows.

I long for sleep in this season
Of changes. For dreams in which the spirits
Of the lost visit, stretching forth their arms
Like the yellowing limbs of willows.

Dear ones, how you blossom
Like the first primitive wildflowers:
Trillium, horsetail, bloodroot.

One theory holds that belief
Derives from these apparitions.
I don't know. I simply welcome
Those faces, tender as buds
Plump with expectation.

Passwords

Select abstractions like Jackson Pollock
Splashes. Consonants, upper, lower cases,
Numerals, ampersands, exclamation points.

The invisible arbiter says weak exhorting
Complexity the way a poet seeks to add
Confusion to approximate profundity

But nothing means what it means to remember
Like your dog's name or your child's.
The street you lived on in the felicity

Of your first marriage or the simple 1-2-3
That hackers discover as easily
As a doorkey over the lintel.

Embrace the inconvenience of looking up
Every time you hope to invade
The ether of porous knowledge.

Or seize upon simplicity
Defying the law of evolution
Like the single-celled creature you long to be.

This morning, our friend, at almost 90
Is worried about the Van Allen Belt
Which contains more catastrophes than

Once imagined. Asteroids and comets of immense
Dimension. Radiance that kills. The laws of chance presume
We're in the path of anguish

And misery. He says there is a plan
To nudge such threats out of orbit with a missile
Or some method still undefined. He hopes to live

To see it. I recall how my father in the years
Before he died, also became obsessed by the vast
Expanse of space, galaxies, quarks, dark

Matter. How he pondered the password
To that panorama of stardust to which he'd soon
Be returning. His identity, at last, stolen.

Crow Song

Off-key in the mortuary of darkness.
What else can you slash
From the world tree. A little
Knowledge is the poison for which
No antidote can be given. Pick up
The leaf, its skeleton reminds you
How the universe flakes off
In a smatter of meteorites. What else
Is there to wish for. Torn ribbons
Of the last romance. The forest
With its undergrowth of kisses.
Lichen on the fallen trunks or moss
Pointing to the north star.
Loss is ordained, why question
The evidence of a footprint,
The body bloating in the sedge.
The quality of mercy versus flesh.
This conundrum. This sideways pass.
This narrow path along the ridge designed
For the surefooted.

Aria

Singing began as a way to capture
Evil spirits. Caught in the cage
Of the larynx to choke on ash
And harmony, desire fills their
Goatish pupils, as if nightingales
Collaborated on a symphony
Or a Chopin mazurka danced
The gaudy excess from their
Bones. Maria Callas lifts her voice
From the ocean where sperm whales
Vocalize, where sirens call
From isolate rocks. Those spirits chained
To the mast begin to tremble, to
Evaporate like ghosts clamped
In a textbook, like a revision
Of Revelations—the pale horse
Whinnying, nodding his head in
Obligation, stamping a hoof
In one drumbeat and now the aria
Begins to soar like a murder of angels
Or demons, like the crows
Hoarse with ambition. Keep singing.
The bars. The grace notes.
The treble clef. And one voice a cappella
To save us.

The Japanese Gardens

Designed by Hoichi Kurisu. Thirty years
In the making. The winding paths
Lead to meditation pools
Where gold, silver and black Koi
Swerve to a sinuous music.

Waterfalls splash into ponds
Where the teahouse shelters
Beneath Scotch Pines rigged
With tension wires to distort
Into full-sized Bonsai trees.
In spring the needles are clipped, the bark
Roughened to expose its ruddy muscle.

A small isle for the master to burn
Incense to honor the ancestors. The boardwalks
Zigzag to forestall demons
Who can only travel in straight lines.

Everything is mastered and ordained.
Each miniature vista: perfect.
My father admired this aesthetic.
Brought us a young bonsai with directions
for its torment that I could not impose.

We rest upon a rough-hewn bench.
The leaves here are turning.
The poplars tremble whispering
Their alias. The sand raked
In crosshatch patterns. The ponds
Deepened so the Koi can overwinter.

The mallards depart
With the first frost. Every winter brings
The axe of ice. Every spring the crews
Remonstrate with acts of nature
Insisting beauty is artifice.

The Herd of Stars

Blue horses rustle the wind
What a night for stars
Jamming the cattle pens

O white heifers, beeves
Your blockheads
Shedding light
And horns hooking
Predictably

The sad harmonica
Quiets your great migration
We dream in small campfires
While you lick salt
Blocks and fatten
On black corn.

How we count on you
Measuring our wealth,
Wish on you
Branded as lovers.

You are crossing dark plains
In the famous drive no talk
Of morning can diminish

Your hooves move over every
Living thing
While we hurl our lariats
Strum our guitars
Following you to slaughter.

Soft Spot

For the woman with sleek knees,
The man with muscled forearms,
The favored child, the Benjamin,
Billie Holliday, Gary Cooper, Casablanca,
The lakeside cottage, Tolstoy, Tosca,
Golden Retrievers, Appaloosas, grilled cheese,
Chocolate milk, old quilts, peonies,
Autumn leaves, pocket watches, honeybees,
Garrison Keillor, Grey's Elegy, Chopin,
The planet Venus, Virginia Woolf, pearls,
Walk-in closets, Monopoly, little sisters,
Porch swings, open windows, new moons,
Charlie Chaplin, Grapes of Wrath, lonely roads,
Hummingbirds, birch trees, first day of school,
Mayan temples, Hershey bars, pinot noir,
Apricots, Isadora Duncan, well-worn jeans,
Flannel pajamas, good sex, luggage with wheels,
First class, first frost, first love,
Crossword puzzles, making lists
Like this, a delicate chasm, the
Fontanel of preferences
That gradually closes, hardens.

Correlations

Because it rained blood that Tuesday
And pigeons cascaded from their roosts
In Atlanta and a tsunami swept away
Two hundred people in Indonesia
As a woman drove over her husband
Because he told her how to vote
And lime trees languished in Key West
Because no snow fell in Philadelphia
And three girls bicycling in Seattle
Vanished because a foundation was dug
For a beach house in Malibu
And two pitbulls were adopted
By an interracial couple from
Atlantic City as a Russian orphan died
Of failure to thrive and a college reunion
Was held at a banquet hall in Indianapolis
Because a man and woman fell in love
In Seoul as another woman walked
By the sea weeping means you and I
Were meant to meet that hot day
With the sidewalks blistering our feet
As we kept on walking.

Cold Prophecies

The weather crewels its gothic designs
Upon glass suborning traction,
Flash fires of dry-ice.

A deadly beauty, white on white
As a child's funeral,
Mass of the Angels.

Spires stud eaves
Like the Night of Long Knives.

Massacred trees,
Bones picked by blackbirds,
Silver-gilt as coffins or frames
Containing landscapes that have stiffened.

Infant cry of the owl haunts
The mind's calm progressions. A hawk
Circles the bitter morning,
Snow-tipped underwings, a cross against the sky.

Homeward

Grey mist sleeves the unfrocked trees.
A season that perpetrates the myth
Of goodwill. An agnostic sky
Low-lidded, obdurate, disenfranchised.

Take the measure of the stars.
A comet dies into the sun
The way a woman slips into the arms
Of an assassin. Knave of love.

Darkness falls early. Farther north
The aurora borealis paints the night
With fluorescence. This is how we learn
To live without the light
Of benevolence.

Tulips

Wood turtles stamp the ground
Like infuriated children to lure
Earthworms, a special treat
Along with slugs, snails and other slimy
Delectables. I feel like stamping
When I observe how he has dug up
The tulip bulbs from a long-established bed,
Scarlet and golden every May,
Because he says, their bloom is brief.
Then there's just these greeny spears
As if warriors left a jungly mess.
He wants all-summer color,
Perennial substance, asks me
If there are varieties of tulips
That bloom through August.
Listen, spring
Is defined with tulips, crocus, iris,
Jonquils, birdsong for gods sake.
That bracelet of velvet tulips.
Black tongues silenced by ignorance.
I think of a neighbor who cut down
A two-hundred year old white oak
So an above-ground plastic pool
Could take its place. The people
Who claim climate change is
A myth, who explain
What god has in mind, at least
For them, who entertain
Notions of trapping wolves and wild
Horses, who lower the educational bar
So everyone can pass, so the world
Can be ruled by idiots. So I can rant

Like a madwoman: O wood turtles
Come out and drum
The land senseless, until the worms
Rise in a slithery mass,
Until everyone understands
The necessity of tulips.

Vanessa Atalanta

Hundreds of Red Admirals flutter,
An extravaganza in the flowering
Crab. Sweet nectar of spring. Migrations
Of the spirit.

Storms to the west
Are greening an ominous sky.
A butterfly lands on my flowered
Shirt. Discovers the error.

I'm discovering what's awry. A month
Early. *Pale Fire* of frost. These docile wings
Need no literary allusions, just stinging
Nettles for spawning.

Their artistry: to shake
Blossoms into surrender
While a tornado watch darkens
The landscape. How it was never
Truth that transfixed beauty,
But fear.

Wild Strawberries

Each year the patch widens
In the abandoned pasture.
Redder than rubies,
Cheerier than garnets
In their tricorne nests
Stemmed to a crested coronet
Where they rest at ease as princesses.

But not royal at all,
Ordinary as a table cloth
Or a pitcher of milk. A tongue
Of sweetness, tiny, not overblown
Like cultivated cousins, they inflame
The field with joyous
Peek-a-boos.

Just underfoot, look down
See where you're stepping next,
Pick one, taste one
This might be the best
Day of your life.

Composing the Essay

The first rule is to narrow the topic
So love becomes unspeakable
As voices buzzing
At the hives of god.

Parse the big sentences
Of justice or mercy
Into soulless abstractions.

Fondle one small creature,
The ferret of imagination
Or the snowy owl of changing weathers

And you will learn that
When the heart fails
Everything fails.

The Coming of Blindness

People become faces, the
Books had no illustrations,
I couldn't see myself in the
Looking glass.
— Jorge Luis Borges

Like blindness, losing each other was gradual
The petals of the white lilacs
Fell softly, vanished
And you held me at arms length
Like newsprint.
The streetlights wore haloes
Of martyrs.

There was a blankness
In the center of making love.
I no longer
Believed our bodies could
Solve equations of loss. We disengaged
To argue over coffee.

Every remark led
To a stupid argument the way
Failing sight makes a man
Stumble over thresholds.
If we had learned Braille,
The language of feeling,
Would anything be different?

Borges says black and red
Are the first colors to be dismissed,
Colors of drama, passion,
Deadly games of challenge.
The blind live
In a luminous greenish mist,
A sort of confusion and grief,
Like this, like this.

Tea Rose

Each week, hand in hand, we journeyed
To the florist to purchase a tea rose
That would float in its glass bowl,
A focus of admiration
On our blue glass coffee table.

Peach edging to gold, deepest pink,
Arterial scarlet, each unfolding its petals
To the fullness of possibility. It was then I learned
How perfection must be transient,
At the edge of anything
Erosion sets its teeth.

I think now of our ritual.
The choosing, how we contemplated
Quality. Celebrating loveliness
That could not last.

You were mindful
Of metaphor. I was a child
Wanting the literal. A rose
Simply a rose.

Bridal Wreath

True name: spirea. But we say
Bridal wreath for the laden branches
Of its blossoms, a heaviness cascading like love or grief.
Promises made with purpose,
Serious as a gravestone that holds the long
Vesture of vows, kept or broken. How these flowers
Weigh the heart with an ambition
To outlast loveliness. How lacking scent, they conjure
The eye of the beholder. The way her dress
Rustled in the spring or the cleft
Of his chin, that first glimpse of accord,
The as-yet-unpossessed sexual intimacy.
The vast bushes stagger beneath
Their finery, their gusto
Of white on white clusters, how life
Enjoins us to grasp abundance,
To grasp and gladden, gorge on brevity.

Apparitions of Earth

Even if you think the earth is hollow
There is no sure way of getting in it
Except by tunneling through solid rock
Or exploring a deep cave
That may have no outlet.

Even if you think the earth is flat
There is no way to prove it.
All evidence denies your theory
Of monsters lurking just off the edge of the map.

In your dream everything might be
The way you want it.
But if you wake thinking the earth is hostile
You're still its child,
Its battered baby.
No court you can imagine
Will hold it responsible
For your bruises, fractures,
Your fatal concussion.

Even if the earth had a door
It would not open
To the cavern of jewels guarded by evil dwarfs
Where the lamp in your hand would provide
Safe passage. Even if that door
Existed it would not wear a sign
Saying Walk Right In
Like a store with a homely bell
Summoning the proprietor from behind
Chintz curtains.

Even if the earth were my body
I could not house you
Or provision you against a future
Full of want.

Glass Lyre Press

exceptional works to replenish the spirit

Glass Lyre Press is an independent literary publisher interested in technically accomplished, stylistically distinct, and original work. Glass Lyre seeks diverse writers that possess a dynamic aesthetic, and an ability to emotionally and intellectually engage a wide audience of readers.

Glass Lyre's vision is to connect the world through language and art. We hope to expand the scope of poetry and short fiction for the general reader through exceptionally well-written books, which evoke emotion, provide insight, and resonate with the human spirit.

Poetry Collections
Poetry Chapbooks
Select Short & Flash Fiction
Anthologies

www.GlassLyrePress.com

www.ingramcontent.com/pod-product-compliance
Lightning Source LLC
Chambersburg PA
CBHW021157080526
44588CB00008B/380